ALAN HARRIS

Alan Harris's other plays include *Sugar Baby* (Dirty Protest);
How My Light Is Spent (Royal Exchange Theatre, Manchester/
Sherman Theatre/Theatre by the Lake; Bruntwood Judges' Prize
2015); *Love, Lies and Taxidermy* (Paines Plough/Sherman
Theatre/Theatr Clwyd); *The Opportunity of Efficiency* (New
National Theatre Tokyo/National Theatre Wales); *The Magic
Toyshop* (Invisible Ink/Theatr Iolo); *The Future for Beginners*
(liveartshow/Wales Millennium Centre); *A Good Night Out in
the Valleys* (National Theatre Wales); *A Scythe of Time* (New
York Musical Theatre Festival); *Cardboard Dad* (Sherman);
Orange (Sgript Cymru). He has also written radio plays for
BBC Radio 4 and Radio 3.

Libretti include *Marsha: A Girl Who Does Bad Things*
(liveartshow/Arcola Grimeborn Festival); *The Hidden Valley*
(Birdsong Opera/Welsh National Opera/Tête à Tête); *The
Journey* (Welsh National Opera); *Rhinegold, Manga Sister*
(both liveartshow/The Yard, London).

Alan Harris

FOR ALL I CARE

NICK HERN BOOKS

London

www.nickhernbooks.co.uk

A Nick Hern Book

For All I Care first published in Great Britain in 2019 as a paperback original by Nick Hern Books Limited, The Glasshouse, 49a Goldhawk Road, London W12 8QP, in association with National Theatre Wales

For All I Care copyright © 2019 Alan Harris

Alan Harris has asserted his right to be identified as the author of this work

Cover design: bwtic.co.uk

Designed and typeset by Nick Hern Books, London
Printed in the UK by Mimeo Ltd, Huntingdon, Cambridgeshire PE29 6XX

A CIP catalogue record for this book is available from the British Library

ISBN 978 1 84842 880 5

Woodland
CARBON
www.woodlandcarbon.co.uk
NICK HERN BOOKS
Printed on Carbon Captured paper

The world premiere of *For All I Care* was commissioned by and first produced by National Theatre Wales in 2018 as part of their NHS70 Season.

For All I Care was performed at Summerhall during the 2019 Edinburgh Festival Fringe and selected to be part of the This is Wales showcase. The company was as follows:

CLARA/NYRI   Hannah Daniel

Director   Jac Ifan Moore
Set & Costume Designer   Carl Davies
Lighting Designer   Katy Morison
Sound Designer   Sam Jones
Emerging Director   Lisa Diveney

Stage Manager   Sarah Thomas
Technical Stage Manager   Lefi Jones
Technician – Relighter   Jason King
Costume Supervisor   Deryn Tudor
Edinburgh Producer   Claire Turner
Associate Producer   Sarah Cole
Emerging Producer   Alice Rush

Characters

CLARA
NYRI

*This play can be performed by one or two actors. In the original
production, it was performed by one actor.*

*This text went to press before the end of rehearsals and so may
differ slightly from the play as performed.*

Clara

It started with winking. I'm lying in bed, listening to Jay-Z on the radio, trying not to think. Then… wink. Never been a winker. More of a blinker. If I try to close one eye the other is destined to follow. You see? I've always thought winking is for people with a swagger and what have I got to swagger about? Nowt.

Now and again my body gives me little messages, in different ways, and this time it happens to be winking.

A Thursday and I'm not thinking but winking. Sweating. It's 7.58 a.m. and I'm dripping. Thirty degrees in Blaenau Gwent in a flat where all the windows are nailed or painted shut. Roasting. Believe me, it's not a home, it's a tomb.

The heat has built up for days and days, something my nan would have called 'too hot for dogs'. Too hot to sleep, too hot for my head, in bed, in a corner of the globe called Green Meadows. Opposite the Flying Start Hub in Sirhowy, you knows? Who ever named it Green Meadows must have been on crack and I'm feeling strange cos of the heat and, on my back, in bed, my naked body stretched out, *Despicable Me* duvet flung long ago onto the brown-and-white Home Bargains rug, I can see the Artex swirls where they should be and my left eye… winks.

Every few seconds my left eye closes and opens without command. Shit. My brain is overheating.

But what can you do or say? Who do you say it to? Put on your sunglasses, have a bowl of Cheerios and prepare for the day.

Today's going to be sticky, tricky, cos of the heat. Look up and out the skylight in the kitchenette, blue canvas in a picture frame. I ponder the challenges of that blue yonder, today, as the kettle struggles to catch up with the heat. I consider some toast but the toaster is broken.

I'm a shoplifter. And hot weather is the pits for shoplifting.

I steal to order for a girl called Diane. Diane scares the shit out of me. You know those types, not big but scary – her calmness makes me wary. Diane is The Devil and she must be obeyed or else she will burn me. Got orders from The Devil for three pairs of leggings, two spangly tops, a mohair jumper and a puffa jacket. In July. Only in Tredegar, I tell you. Dare not come back with anything less than the list. Diane hosts a get-together every week at her red-brick semi – sort of an Ann Summers party for shoplifted goods. She even puts on a golden spread of food stolen from M&S in Friar's Walk.

I look out on to the back, and through my sunglasses I can see the world is melting. A blue-and-white van with high-backed sides scours the street for any old iron – a skinny lad jumps out and picks up a discarded radiator. Hot metal.

Today is definitely a day for stealing swimwear.

But no one wants swimwear in Tredegar, I tell you.

Say what you will about me but I do not shit on my own doorstep. I goes to Newport or Merthyr or Aberdare or anywhere to pinch, to source Diane's list I'll go that extra inch, yard, mile.

I met someone once who said they 'believed' in shoplifting because it's a form of redistribution. Direct action against the corporations. Do me a favour. There speaks someone who is not truly skint.

I don't believe in anything because I can't afford to. Not God or any sort of religion or people or kindness or Santa Claus or most of our laws or the power of face cream or that eating more vegetables is good for you.

Believing in stuff is pointless.

Before I leave the house I spy my tablets on the table – have I taken them today? I think so…

I walk to the bus stop – down Chartist Way – and step onto the X4 to Ebbw Vale in the shadow of Lidl. Two girls at the back start to giggle and I ignore, taking off my sunglasses cos I think it's rude not to see people's eyes when you speak to them. But that's a mistake as the driver asks:

Why you winking at me?

I'm not.

You just did.

Look, just give me a single to Ebbw Vale, yeah? Any chance I can have half?

How old are you?

Eighteen but I'm saving up to buy a Lamborghini.

Driver gives me half single.

As soon as I sit I know the day is far too bright for me; no way can it be this hot for so long in Tredegar. It's like someone's turned up the contrast on the telly and the remote is lost down the back of the settee.

As we trundle through Rhyd y Blew one minute I'm thinking about KFC – advertising really works on me – and the next moment I get a sign.

I'd almost forgotten about the signs, hadn't had one in four months but there it is.

The sign, basically, says:

Today, Clara, you should kill yourself.

I know. Charming.

Every once in a while I'd like to get a good sign, like: 'Nice shoes Clara' but no, they're always telling me stuff I know I shouldn't do.

10.07 a.m. Changing room. Peacocks. Ebbw Vale. There's no Loss Prevention Officer (can you believe that's what they call security nowadays?) and the woman who looks after the changing rooms couldn't give a toss about loss so I take in ten items.

I'm struggling to get all the clothes on and now she's taking an interest, this woman who looks after the changing rooms.

You okay in there, love?

I'm wearing four pairs of leggings, two vests, a cardigan and that mohair jumper. I'm sweating buckets.

Yeah, all good. I'm terrible with decisions, thank you.

Do you need a second opinion?

No, not right now.

I wonder: Where'm I gonna stuffa the puffa? Not sure if it's the heat or the constant fucking winking or this surge of mania or the woman standing outside or the fact I'm dressed for an assault on Narnia but I can't get the sign that told me to kill myself out of my head.

Have you ever had an out-of-body experience, madam?

Try to avoid them if you can.

I'm looking down on the cubicle, I'm up there and I see myself setting light to the mohair. I'm expecting it go woooooooomf but no, surprisingly, mohair jumpers do not catch light that easily. I know. I'm standing there and the flames on the mohair are spreading slowly and the woman shouts:

You smoking in there?

I am – but not in the way she means.

The smoke alarm goes off and she draws back the curtain and by now the mohair is fully alight – I'm starting to go up on my own Peacocks pyre – and I see this woman who looks after the changing rooms throw up her arms in the air and shriek:

She's on fire!

Then she leaves.

The flames get higher.

She comes back with an extinguisher.

You okay, love? You was properly on fire. I think you banged your head when I sprayed you with the foam. Just lie back. Ambulance is on the way.

The paramedics stretcher me out of Peacocks. One of them asks:

Can you tell us your name, darlin'?

Clara Bright.

Is there anyone we can call, darlin'?

No.

We're going to take good care of you, darlin'.

Thank you.

Is this puffa jacket yours, darlin'?

(CLARA *manages a weak nod.*)

I wink. I think:

This is an extreme way to shoplift from Peacocks.

It turns out it's illegal to try to commit suicide by burning yourself to death in stolen clothes in a Peacocks changing room. Just in case you were wondering.

After they treat my minor burns on my tummy, establish I have no mummy, they take me to this new secure-unit thingy. Poked and prodded, mentally and physically, and my AMHP questions me about health and wealth and well-being and did I have any pets and what's my flat like and do I have any family and how often do I eat and do I take my tablets daily and I'm semi-honest with the answers and I sign a form for something and the reason I sign is that this place seems a better fit than my shitty bedsit. I get my own room. Room number eight. The AMHP sees a line of ugly red blotches on my arm.

Do you self-harm, Clara?

I can't tell her the truth about those blotches so I fudges it.

They're nothing – I think I'm allergic to mohair.

Following day I'm taken to court, Newport, and the magistrate woman says I'm to return to the secure unit, for my own good like, and I'm happy enough with that. Not clappy happy but what can you do?

She asks me:

Why did you do it?

And I tells her.

I gets signs, your worship. That day, while on the bus, we passed KFC, you know the one near Morrisons in Rhyd, and then we pass that little chapel where the bus turns right?

I can see she's never caught the bus in her life.

There was a message for me on the billboard thing outside the chapel. It said:

'If you believe that two hundred million people are going to fly up to heaven and be greeted by Jesus why not get ahead of the crowd and kill yourself today?'

I have one more thing to say to the beak before she ships me back to the unit:

I'm not winking at you on purpose, your honour.

Nyri

It's too hot to stay in bed any longer.

I roll over and I can only open one eye.

I should have taken my make-up off last night. I peel the other eye open. Lying next to me is a man. Constable Alex Collins.

A policeman I slept with last night.

Lying with one leg hanging out the bed he looks like a junior copper – doesn't look old enough to deal with the idiots around here.

As I slip on my pants I catch a sight of myself bent double in the reflection of the bedroom window. I look like my fucking mother.

Alex's front door closes with a soft and satisfying click and I make myself two promises – one of them is not to sleep with policemen half my age again.

The other is to do the thing I've been putting off for the past month.

The morning air is already sticky. This is the tenth hot day in a row – must be some kind of Welsh record.

Now, where the fuck am I?

Church Street. The houses just down from the old Central Surgery?

How did you get there, Nyri? I hear you ask. Thank you.

It started with a quick drink in The Castle with a load of nurses who mostly work at YAB (for those not from round here, that's Ysbyty Aneurin Bevan). That descended into a bitching session into how the NHS is falling apart around our ears – and who was to blame. I learnt a song by someone called Captain SKA?

(She sings a couple of lines from the second verse of 'Liar Liar' by Captain SKA.)

Yeah, a bit on the nose but… it's a good tune.

Then down the hill, on to Cambrian and The Olympia for three-for-one cocktails (I do love a 'Spoons) and a load of coppers come in. We know them – everyone in Tredegar who wears a uniform knows each other.

I've had enough by eleven – we're in The Loft – I'm at that point in the night when it's either go home or be sick in your handbag when Alex says to me:

You can crash at mine, babe.

Really – he'd called me babe – and I think: I'm going to see you naked.

I text Joshy, my son, he's fifteen, and tell him I've been asked to pick up an extra shift. He replies with two letters – O and K.

Wow, you don't get many mornings as bright as this in Blaenau Gwent.

I pick up a coffee and a Steak Bake from Greggs in the arcade and walk towards home.

My shift starts at noon. I'm on twelve till twelve? I've worked at a 'new' mental-health unit near YAB for three years.

As I slink down Commercial my hangover kicks in and I'm hoping I can get home without seeing anyone I know.

Fat chance in Tredegar.

Hiya, Nyri – you're coming from the wrong way.

Marco Grigson. My boss.

My hangover is really kicking in.

Thought you lived thatta way, Nyri.

Been to Greggs. Fancied a Steak Bake.

Oh right. Warm enough for you?

I pull open my top and let it flap to show how warm I am – I get a waft of body odour that stinks of sweat and a lack of deodorant. I think Marco can smell the sex on me.

An awkward pause where Marco wants to say 'you been out all night' and I want to tell him to mind his own fucking business.

You go out last night?

Quiet drink.

Anywhere nice?

No.

You did go somewhere but it was shite?

I had once opened up to Marco and it was a big mistake. A month ago my mum, Mary, died. Cancer. Liver first, then brain. Marco asked how I was coping so I told him. I told him she had the first round of chemo and that made her ill. I also told him it was the radiotherapy that hurt her. They put Mary back on the chemo after but she couldn't take it. It only made her life a misery for the last three months. I insisted Mary, my own mother, went into hospital – best place for her in the circumstances – when all Mary had wanted was to die at home. The care she had was fantastic, the very essence of the word 'care' and I spent hours upon hours sitting next to her, holding her hand, listening to her breathing.

I remember thinking it seemed the breaths out were longer than the breaths in.

Then, all of a sudden, she stopped breathing.

No great speeches or smiles or hugs or kisses or last messages like on the TV or films. That's how people die, isn't it; they just stop.

All Mary wanted was to die at home and I denied her that.

Marco was sympathetic – he put his hand on my shoulder, here, and now Marco feels he can say anything to me.

Listen, Marco, I got to go, I'll see you later.

Aren't those the same clothes you were wearing yesterday at work? Where you really been this morning?

So I tells him:

I've been fucking a policeman half my age, Marco.

That shut him up.

I'm hoping Joshy's gone to school when I finally get home – me and him live in Cefn Rhos? – but I hear the TV as I slip into the hallway; BBC News, some politician patronising Naga Munchetty about the 'real-terms' increase in funding for the NHS.

I decide to brazen it out.

All right, Joshy? You okay?

Standard teenager response (no reply). But there's something else…

A girl's voice.

As I open the living-room door I've obviously caught Josh and a girl doing something they shouldn't be doing.

Not that.

Hi, uh, Mam, didn't think you'd be back till… this is Diane.

You know some girls look normal but, underneath, you know
they are dog rough?

That's 'Diane' for you.

Josh's sitting on the floor. Diane standing above him. When
I come in the room it looks as though he's putting the rug
back down.

All right, Mrs…

She doesn't know my last name.

I'll be upstairs, Joshy.

*Right you are, Mam, we're just watching TV. I've left some
washing on the kitchen floor, is that okay?*

Shouldn't you be going to school?

A smirk from Diane.

Just about to, Mam.

Believe it or not, this is the most Josh has spoken to me in
weeks. It seems like only yesterday he was happy to hold my
hand while walking round M&S but now my main role seems to
be feeding him and washing his clothes.

I'll be upstairs – in your nan's room, clearing out her shit.

This is the thing I've been meaning to do for the past month.

I stand before the door with a roll of black bags in one hand and
a strong black coffee in the other.

It's more difficult to go in than I imagined it would be – I half-
expect when I push open the door she'll be there, Mary, lying in
bed, barking orders or complaining that her arse is itching.

But she's not there.

Another mouthful of coffee and I make a start, I'm finally
clearing out the last of my mother.

Two hours I've cleared the make-up and the clothes – the ones
I can still see her wearing, some I've never clapped eyes on.

The socks, the bedsocks, the tights, the knickers and bras, forty years' worth of coats – she loved a coat. I find sixty quid in the pocket of a lime-green jacket.

Black bags filled with Mary's life pile up, barring the door, trapping me in till I've cleared out the lot. In fact there are two piles – 'charity', 'not charity'.

Now for the boxes on top of the wardrobe.

A collection of thimbles – charity.

A collection of bank cards, special-offer coupons and store debit cards. Not charity. An old-school Walkman and an Orange mobile phone that weighs a ton – charity.

A folder of household bills. Not charity.

A folder from work – instructions to matrons in 1980 about how to stop the spread of infection.

A massive folder on new clinical procedures for ward nurses 1978.

A folder on new clinical procedures for ward nurses 1985.

A folder on new clinical procedures for ward nurses 1991.

A folder on new clinical procedures for ward nurses 2000.

A folder on new clinical procedures for ward nurses 2006.

A bunch of old pictures – the top one is my mum, she looks about seventeen, with a group of girls who look straight out of nursing college? Looks like they're standing on the steps of the old town hall. In the middle, taller than all, is Nye Bevan.

I might frame that.

Pictures of us on holiday – when Dad was alive, Tenby? I think that's me in a pram...

A slim folder with –

(NYRI *gets out a folded-up piece of paper. She holds it up*.)

This is the thing that sets me off?

Not one tear. Not even a lump in my throat. Until this.

(*She reads the leaflet.*)

'Your new National Health Service begins on 5th July. It will provide you with all medical, dental and nursing care. Everyone – rich or poor, man, woman or child – can use it or any part of it. There are no charges – except for a few special items. There are no insurance qualifications. But it is not a "charity". You are all paying for it, mainly as taxpayers, and it will relieve your money worries in time of illness.'

You know, most mothers read bedtime stories to their kids?

My memory is being on my mother's knee in the living room – we were living in New Tredegar then. On Duffryn Terrace? And she, my mother, would read this leaflet to me. She's the nurse and I pretend to be the patient.

I had some wonderful illnesses in New Tredegar.

Red-spotted tongue or my insides were jelly that wasn't set.

And she cures me.

Without charge.

I'd assumed this scrap of paper had been lost a long time ago.

But it's here, she kept it right here for all this time.

Not charity.

Where does the time go? Huh?

Shower, shit, teeth, change, bowl of All Bran, off to work.

I don't drive so I usually catch the bus – society's great divide: those who ride the bus and those who don't.

Clara

Have you ever stayed in a medium-secure unit for people with mental disorders?

I can tell you they are, above all else, boring.

You spend hours doing nothing. A dozen people in their own rooms too frightened to talk to each other. Brother, we all know we're in there for something mad and no one really wants to acknowledge that.

So I settles back, thinking about something to eat, and watches a repeat of *The Chase* on ITV2 – it's the one I'd like to go up against the least, you know, The Beast? when lunch arrives.

What you doing here?

Came to bring you your grub – your waitress for the day. I think it's eggs.

How did you...?

The woman on the desk, Hilary, is my cousin – we used to go to Barry Island together when we was kids. Hilary said it would be okay for me to bring you your meal. She liked the idea. Good for you to connect, Clara, yeah?

Diane holds a tray, a plate with a plastic cover to protect the food. Next to the plate is six packets of salt and next to that a blackcurrant slushie. I know what's coming.

Diane moves a magazine out the way, puts down the tray.

The girls have been asking for you, Clara. You was missed last week. Senora was gutted not to get her mohair jumper.

Sorry 'bout that – I got into a bit of a tizz. What you doing here, Diane?

Come to see how you are. What mates do.

There's nothing I can get. No drugs, nothing.

Said I come to see how you are.

Really?

Do I lie, Clara? I keeps my word. It's important to keep your word.

Her voice is level and I know this is going to end badly – she's The Devil – and I looks around the room, hoping there's a sign that says 'stick that fork in Diane's neck now' but there's nothing. The Chaser gets a question wrong. The clock ticks. I winks.

Skinny jeans, a floral pom-pom-trim dress from New Look, an Ophira Feather Flower crossbody bag from Topshop – the orders are piling up, Clara.

I can't get out of here, Diane, there's no way I can.

Diane takes a slurp of her slushie. I can see her tongue has turned dark blueishy.

Hold out your arm, Clara.

Diane is The Devil and you have to do what The Devil says.

She drains the last of the slushie and off pops the top, spilling the ice out on to the duvet.

You needs a reminder of how much we misses you and loves you, yeah?

Diane rips open a packet of salt and places its contents on my forearm. Then another and a third. A large chunk of ice. Not nice.

You heard of the salt and ice challenge? It's a YouTube sensation. People normally film it but we don't do that.

Diane holds the ice to the salt on my forearm.

Clara, you got to learn.

Nothing happens.

Then it does.

It starts to burn.

Nyri

Clara's not in her room. I find her on the roof, smoking.

You're Clara Bright, aren't you?

She gives me a wink.

Look, really, you shouldn't be up here.

I'm not going to jump. You can see for miles from up here – is that Festival Park over there?

Maybe we should go down.

Maybe you should chill out. I'm only having a fag for crying out loud.

As your nurse I've a responsibility –

Sorry?

I work here. Nyri.

That's a funny name. Nyri.

I was named after, never mind. You can keep the cigs but I'll have to take the lighter, yeah? Where did you get it from?

I'll finish this and come in. Yeah?

Please, let's go back down.

It's too hot in my room, hoping there was breeze up here. Gasping for a fag. Want one?

I take a smoke from Clara.

You looks tired, Nyri – you wants to book yourself in here, it's very relaxing. Have you ever considered setting fire to yourself?

Do you have any family, Clara?

None to speak of.

I drop my fag on the roof, twist it into the gravel with the sole of my Sketchers.

Look, we really should go down.

*Am I going to get in trouble? You going to tell that boss fella
I was up here?*

You can trust me, Clara.

Promise?

I won't tell.

*Can I leave the unit? I need to go to Newport for some stuff.
Ebbw Vale town centre at a push.*

*Section 17 of the Mental Health Act says you can leave the
ward for short periods of time under certain circumstances.*

And they are?

Believe me, you don't qualify. Come on.

Clara

I can see nurse Nyri wants to chat but, matter of fact, she's got
some big meeting to go to. I act like I don't care, this is all
normal fare, I'm going to settle in here, chill out in my home
from home, enjoy the telly, white blankets and chrome.
Anything I can get you, Clara? Consider asking for a diamond
tiara but settle on something I'm really missing, from the bedsit.
Can you do that for me, Nyri? She's at a bit of a loss, she'll
have to ask the boss.

Nyri

The meeting is not going in the direction I want it to – like
a supermarket trolley with a wonky wheel.

*What do you mean she's not 'medium', Marco? She is, she
clearly is. This is a girl with a neuro-development disorder.*

Marco isn't hearing me. He's one of those people who has a sort
of smile across his face whenever he pretends to listen to you.

I think he thinks it makes him likeable.

It doesn't.

He's also one of these people who constantly clicks their pen,
you know?

Click, click, click.

*I don't like this any more than you do, Nyri, but there it is. If she
could afford it she'd be in a better position to –*

She's not BUPA material, Marco.

My hands are tied.

*We can't do this – we have a responsibility to the patient. We
have a responsibility to make her life better, whatever it takes.*

Click, click, click.

*She hasn't done anything out of the ordinary while with us?
Nothing dangerous?*

Depends what you call dangerous.

Again with the smile.

Click click.

Is this the NHS we want, Marco?

Sorry?

Is this the NHS we would like?

*It's the one we've got, Nyri – now if that's all, I've a
procurement meeting to go to.*

*This young person, Clara, has made four attempts on her life –
that we know about.*

*To be fair, we don't know if those were serious attempts or cries
for help.*

She set fire to herself in Peacocks!

Click, click.

With that he makes a note in his notebook, nods, looks me in
the eye, says:

*We'll leave her for now, let her sleep tonight, make a final
decision as soon as poss.*

*If we send that girl back out there we are sentencing her to
death. She will kill herself.*

*I don't want to go over this again, Nyri, but she has been
assessed as low risk – a risk to herself and not to the general
public – therefore she has to be looked after in a low-security
facility. We are a medium-secure facility. We cannot find any
beds in any low-security unit in Wales and, believe me, we have
tried. We've even asked over the border – the bed is just not
there for her at this precise time. We are hoping that will change
but until then… You know the pressure we're under here.*

*She's not some bed-blocker, Marco, who's waiting to go into The
Rookery – she has serious mental-health issues.*

*Taking up a bed when there is a list of people we need to look
after in this medium unit. It's just… logistics.*

Jesus Christ, the world has gone fucking mad.

I'll take that into consideration, Nyri.

With that Marco smiles, closes his notebook, gives his silver
Parker pen a final click click and gets up from his chair.

*She's asked me to fetch her something from her flat, is that
'acceptable'?*

He puts his hand on my shoulder, here.

I know you feel guilty about the way your mother died, Nyri, but you musn't blame yourself. You can't save everyone, Nyri.

Then the fucker leaves – I can still feel his handprint burning into my shoulder.

Sometimes as a nurse, despite all the crap, you know you're doing a good thing. But sometimes you feel a bit helpless. It gets you here, you know, just here, you can feel it.

Clara

I hear the door creak creak and a little nursey cough. I keep my eyes closed, my breathing level and try a little snore. She closes the door and walks away. Score.

Nyri

Hunting for Clara's pyjamas in her bedsit is like looking for a shit in a shitstack. I try to open a window to let out some of the funk but it won't budge. I saw a documentary recently about 'troubled' teens who are sent to prison for a week. Shock tactics? One of the kids cries a lot. Any time I sees teens on the telly I think 'How would my Joshy cope with that?' I look around this place and wonder how would anyone cope with this?

Clara

The door (creak creak) and that little nursey cough. Something placed at the bottom of my bed and raising my head I consider shouting after her 'These aren't my PJs' but, instead, put the M&S cotton to my cheek. The tag says they're from the Cool Comfort range? Why does a gift of new pyjamas feel so strange?

Nyri

The house is quiet when I get in.

Joshy has left most of the lights on – nothing unusual there, and I think about having a cuppa before bed. I'm not going to sleep anyway. I take the brew through to the living room and switch on the news. BBC Wales. One of their special reports on the state of the NHS – where they go around Wales and ask people stuff? I think they do it cos they fancies a trip out of Cardiff. The front gate of the hospital in Llantrisant, one of the junior doctors is talking to the skinny newsreader – you knows the one with the dark hair who always looks as though she's dressed up for a night out... Anyway, this doctor is not holding back:

They promise us a properly funded service with enough doctors and nurses. But, we, on the front line, know that's a fantasy. The NHS is understaffed and underfunded. As a clinician I believe in evidence – yes, facts and figures and what I see every day. At a time of extreme financial pressure we have to ask ourselves whether it is viable to stretch our NHS even further when we can't manage properly at the moment. It's crazy, yes?

Lucy nods like she's the one with lives in her hands – not just a BBC microphone.

Then it hits me something's wrong. The rug in front of the telly, it's pointing the wrong way. I know it's pointing the wrong way because when I put it down I put the creamier bit towards the telly where less people will walk on it. Makes sense, yeah?

I lift up the rug, the parquet flooring is uneven, you know the wood blocks? I take up one block, then another. Below them is a hole and in the hole is a Tesco carrier bag.

In the bag is a load of other bags – in each is four small white tablets. Each has AB1960 written in small letters on one side. I take one of the packets and place the rug back.

Just gone 2 a.m. I get out my ageing iPhone.

Have you just finished your shift?... will you pick me up... yeah, I'll be on the corner of the street.

I watch Alex sleep in the morning. His breath is even. The ins as long as the outs.

I don't sneak out this time but, instead, make coffee and toast and jam as he stretches into the kitchen, dressed in a pair of those jockey-type pants and fuck-all else. It's going to be another hot one today.

I put the little bag of pills on the table.

Do you know what these are, Alex?

Some kind of drug?

Yes, but do you know exactly...

Could be anything.

I found them. Last night. Underneath my living-room rug. My son put them there – him and his, well, I don't even know if she's his girlfriend.

Is he using them?

Don't know.

Asked him?

He's a teenager. To be honest, I hardly see him these days.

Your son is probably a drug dealer, Nyri. Want me to have a word?

Are you going to arrest him?

Do you want me to?

I'll have a think on my way to work. So, what do you think they are?

Take one. Really. Take one and you'll soon know what it is.

Clara

I lie on my bed (I've taken my meds) and let my mind wander out the unit, along the road, the gate and up to the real hospital. People everywhere. In my Cool Comfort PJs I look down from a great height, looks like a city. A city of ants.

I realise as I watch all the people in the hospital busy and strive, that it's the ants that are keeping this place alive.

I don't believe in anything but in that moment, for some reason, I believe Nyri wants the best for me.

But The Devil's out there. Her horns are glowing and her shopping list is growing.

Nyri

I'd noticed the marks on Clara's arm when we were on the roof having a fag but thought it best not to mention it while she has the chance to jump fifty feet down.

Her room seems safer ground.

It's nothing. It's the ice-and-salt challenge. You ever done it?

What, burn myself?

It's all over YouTube. Diane says we should put it up but –

Diane?

Uh, yeah, she visited me yesterday.

You had a visitor? It wasn't in the book.

Her cousin's the woman on the door.

Hilary? This Diane, what she look like? Red hair?

Yeah.

Dyed red hair?

Like a downmarket version of Rita Ora.

That's her, Clara. You know her?

I knows her.

You know her well enough for her to visit you here?

Never invited her.

Is she a drug dealer?

That. And more.

I hand Clara a pencil and a pad.

I knows you knows it, please, write down Diane's address for me.

I don't expect her to write but…

I swipe out of the unit.

Hilary is picking her nose.

I go to Bedwellty Gardens. I'm not sure where it is so I google it. Diane's doing all right for herself. I tell the cab not to wait, this might take a while. As I go through the garden gate I think this Diane can't be that bad – she has a set of ornamental frogs leading to her front door.

A deep breath and hammer the door which opens too quickly.

What you doing here?

Um, Diane, I'm Joshy's… Josh's mother, remember me?

Did he tell you where I lives?

No, no, that's not… I think these belong to you.

I hold out the bag of pills which Diane doesn't take.

Also, while I'm at it, Clara Bright is my patient.

Aaaaah, Clara.

Don't come near either of them again. Okay?

Or what?

Or – just that. You got that?

I look at the bag in my palm and then, as I look back up, something speeds towards my face.

Diane's fist.

Stagger backwards. I clear my vision, a drop of blood seeps from my nose and lands on one of the frogs.

I wish I'd told the cab to wait.

You tell Clara I'm coming for her.

Clara

As I open my blinds on another too-hot morning, the boss man enters my room and perches on the bed. I hear click, click, click. His pen. That's annoying.

The sun streams in – I'm a tomato in a greenhouse, turning redder by the second. He's holding a clipboard, he's about to open his trap when Nyri appears. She has a large plaster over her nose.

She says she doesn't want to talk about it. Just a little accident. With a tone she says 'Thought you said you'd call me if you were going to speak to Clara, Marco?'

They look at each other the way two cats might. Fight?

I've some news. Things have progressed.

Click, click.

I frown. I wink. I'm about to say, do you think we can pull the blinds down when he says:

We need to move you, Clara.

Nyri

I know what's going on here – Marco's a sneaky fucker.

Where she going? Another room? Is Vijay on the end going home?

We need Clara's bed.

She's using her bed.

A decision has been made to move her to a low-security unit.

Great. Where she going?

Nowhere. That's the problem. There is no bed for her. Therefore, she will be sent home. A care package will be put in place where Clara can be an outpatient. It's a clinical decision. Sorry, no, it's not. That's a lie. We just need the bed and there's no other bed in low security. Anywhere.

You can't just let her fend for herself.

She is considered a risk to herself but not to the public – that risk can be managed in the community.

Community? Managed? Are you shitting me?

Clara

I look down as he's holding out the clipboard. I can't
concentrate on the words.

*I don't know if Nyri has explained this to you but we feel, with
careful support, it's best if you go home. Isn't that great news?
We have to make a few arrangements and in the meantime I'll
leave you in Nyri's capable hands – you've got a good one
there. A wink isn't enough, Clara – you need to sign this.*

He hands me his silver pen. Is this a trick?

Click, click.

I take off my sunglasses as it's rude not to look people in the
eyes and the contrast in the room is so dense the blues have
merged with the reds.

Click, click.

Boss man smiles a smile without any warmth – an achievement
in this heat.

Blinded by the light, I move an inch towards him, but can't see
the words on the page and he's got me in his sights, I can't fight
his might.

I sign.

Nyri

Back at home, I sit in the armchair across from the telly, a
packet of peas balanced on my nose. There's nothing more I can
do for Clara. Only one thing for it – I slip the little white tablet
on my tongue and swallow and… after twenty minutes nothing
has happened – I feel exactly the same. Maybe they're just
vitamins… As I remove the peas I notice the picture of Mam on
the steps of the town hall on the shelf but there's something
missing. Or, rather, someone. A slight cough snaps my head to
the left and Nye Bevan is standing in my living room.

You okay, young lady? That looks nasty. Your nose?

Uh, yeah, Mr Bevan, hi, just an accident.

*I thought politics was a blood sport – maybe it's nursing these
days.*

Can I… get you a cup of tea?

*In a minute. You're in a right pickle, aren't you? You'd like to
care but you can't.*

Clara? What can I do?

*You know, Nyri – fantastic name by the way – it's easy to say
'I believe in the good, the beautiful, the true.' But what does
that mean?*

Not sure what you're getting –

*The problem is always more immediate and particular. You
could say you believe in doing your duty.*

I do –

*Life would be easy, wouldn't it, if it was always clear what your
duty was. You're a pawn in this game, Nyri.*

Thanks. What's your point, Mr Bevan?

*Usually there's a conflict between duty and loyalty. In order to
serve one you have to abandon the other.*

I've got to abandon either duty or loyalty?

*There's more to it than that – shall we have that cup of tea
before I really get started?*

Clara

The boss man click-clicks and I wink-wink and think about what's waiting for me out there. I put on my sunglasses against the glare when Nyri skids through the door.

Nyri

I'm not giving up on her, Marco.

Sorry?

I made a commitment to care for her and I'm going to do that. And, anyway, I was told that I have a duty to care for her.

By who?

Nye Bevan.

I unfurls a folded-up brown leaflet.

Do you know what this is? Do you, Marco?

I'm not sure how this is relevant.

'Your new National Health Service begins on 5th July. It will provide you with all medical, dental and nursing care. Everyone – rich or poor, man, woman or child – can use it or any part of it.'

What's that got to do with…?

I'm taking care of her, Marco.

We've done all we can.

I'm taking her home.

What? Don't be stupid. You can't take her home.

I'm stupid? Grab your puffa jacket, Clara, you're coming with me.

This is… this is ridiculous. It's crazy.

It's what we're meant to do, Marco.

'What we're meant to do'? What world are you living in, Nyri?

I can look after her.

That's not the point. Please wait there, young lady, Nyri, the hall – I need a word in private.

I'm taking her home, Marco. We're going to live in a civilised society.

You can't save them all, Nyri.

Try stopping me. I've got a spare room.

Clara

And I believe.

I believe in Nyri.

Click, click fucking click.

Out the room in a shot, hand in hand with Nyri, she swipes the door, fresh air! The boss man shouts down the hall, Hilary stands like a stone statue, a rock-still pose, finger up her nose, and into the sunlight, I'm expecting to take a turn towards the car park but she doesn't own a motor and we head for the bus stop, over a low wall and the boss man follows us out and I hear his shout (something about discipline) and up pulls this car, the guy winds down a window and: 'Want a lift, girls?' Nyri says 'Drive. Far. Away.' Fucking hell, we're making a getaway in a police car.

It's a wonderful home. It has wonderful flowers in the front garden and wonderful wooden floors beyond the wonderful red front door. The wonderful hall carpet that runs up the stairs – it's held in place by small brass-rod things – and on to the landing. Nyri stops and pushes open a door to a wonderful bedroom and I go in. It's... wonderful.

This, uh, used to be my mother's room.

Did she die in that bed?

Unfortunately no. Can I get you anything, Clara?

Can we open the windows?

Windows open. A room where nothing is broken. The heat that has been building up has somewhere to go.

I sleep – for sixteen hours. You know one of those sleeps where you don't even get up for a wee? When I do, the soap smells of mango.

I go downstairs and there's a lad sitting on the breakfast bar, I think I've seen him in Spar and I say good day but he just tuts and rolls his headphone-covered head, moving away, hallway, front door, out.

I have toast with honey, peanut butter and jam and Nutella. Stellar. Nyri enters.

Eat whatever you want. Oh, you have.

It's probably the first time I've seen Nyri smile.

Nyri asks how does this feel to me?

Nyri

During the night I pop my head in to check on Clara. In fact I set my alarm for every two hours so I can see that she's okay. She sleeps right through the night and I find her in the kitchen. As Clara closes the fridge door I see the hint of a smile.

I ask her how she feels and she tells me she feels at home, back to bed.

I take a call from Marco, a warning that I'm putting my whole future in jeopardy, and then I sit next to her on the bed and

Clara leans in to me, like this. I cradle her head in this part of
my neck and she does something I don't expect; she cries. I tell
her there's no need to cry and sense that there is, there's every
need to cry so I let her get on with it.

*I've got to go out this morning – something I have to do today –
but when I get back we'll have lunch, yes, Clara?*

This makes her cry more.

I've got to go out now, Clara, see you in a bit.

I'm picked up at the corner of our street.

One of the great advantages of sleeping with a policeman is you
can ask for favours.

Not that kind of favour.

On a clear and bright Tuesday morning we head for Bedwellty
Gardens.

Clara

A clear and bright Tuesday morning. The boss man won't leave
her be. Before she goes out Nyri has a one-sided phone
conversation, defence rather than attack – I know she knows
how to give it back but yes, she knows what this means, yes,
she knows they could take me forcibly, yes, she knows it could
be the end of her career, yes, she knows, she knows, she knows
how serious this is. But not once does she apologise.

Flog It is on the telly and as I watch they agonise over the
future of a brass dog – it's got them thinking – I realise that I'm
not winking. I have not winked since I entered this house.

I wander the rooms. A picture of Nyri and the lad Josh on some
sort of ride – Alton Towers? – and I can see how alike they look
in glee.

A silver-framed picture of a black-and-white nurse standing on some steps with a black-and-white older man who looks as though he's good at telling jokes.

I drift into the front room as the telephone chimes and click-click. The sound of the boss man's voice makes me sick.

Uh, yeah, Ny? You there? Pick up… It's Marco. Again. Look, this has to stop. This isn't helping anyone. I'm only thinking of you. If this goes on any longer I can't cover this up, I have to get in touch with Marisa at the Health Board and… I'm only thinking of you, you know that, right?

Click-click.

And I knows.

Deep down I knows.

All I want is to live in a house where the toaster works and you can open the windows. Is that too much to ask?

I knows.

I knows care when I sees it. When I feels it. I knows that last night I slept in a proper home and even though it feels like a future it's not my future. It can't be Nyri's future. The world needs as many good nurses as it can get – not one less. I guess.

Nyri

Diane's surprised to see me at her weekly party – along with four uniforms and a trading-standards official. It's an Aladdin's Cave of stolen gear and outlawed designer drugs in a semi-detached.

(Right now) she's awaiting sentence in Swansea for handling stolen goods, theft and dealing.

She didn't mention anything about Joshy and he's never mentioned her to me.

On the way back home, I tell Alex I might be the one he's nicking next. The girl from the hospital? he asks. Yup, I've technically kidnapped her. He says if he gets the call to arrest me he'll tip me off, give me a head start. Head start or not he'll probably find me waiting on the fucking bus stop. He laughs his best carefree laugh.

Clara

At least she gave me one night in a home with sweet-smelling soap, a glimmer of hope.

Hilary's surprised to see me at the unit and ushers me to the waiting room. She waits as I wait till the boss man comes through. Click-click. I tell him this was Nyri's idea, my return, she had no idea the trouble it would cause, she's very sorry and smile and click-click.

Everything's going to be okay. Apparently. Every day someone will see me at the flat and check my medication and my weight and ask and reassure, just to make sure. He asks me how I feel and I say on a scale of one to ten it's a seven. Heaven, in fact, and I'm only sweating cos of the heat. Do I want to take off my puffa? Not just yet, thankya.

Thank you for helping me to help you, Clara.

Right back at ya, you fucka.

Everything's going to be just fine, Clara.

Click-click.

And... I... wink.

Shit.

He won't be two shakes of a lamb's tail, without fail, no need to make a song and dance, arrange transport, then we can get you home. In the waiting room, I survey the space and I start a little coughing fit. I ask Hilary if she can get me a drink of water? She oughta stay but I tells her I'm burning up. She's only too pleased to fulfil my order.

Alone in the waiting room I consider what has to happen. I know I can't stay here. I know I can't go back to the bedsit. I have no choices. I know what I have to do – and this is the perfect place to do it.

Nyri

The unit is being rebuilt after the fire.

The investigation found that it was a breach of regulations that no one searched Clara's puffa jacket for a lighter when she came back. That was Hilary's job. She's been suspended.

It has been definitely decided that Clara is 'medium', a risk to herself and the general public.

She burned down the whole mental-health unit in Ebbw Vale to prove it.

They found her a bed – in Wrexham. That's normally an issue with young people being so far away from their families but in Clara's case…

On the train journey up there I sit and watch the Welsh countryside go by and wonder if I'm the closest thing Clara has to a family. Isn't that sad?

I'm struggling to see where the line separating the patients from the rest of us is but, then again, we're all patients at some time or another, aren't we?

Clara's in room number four.

I go in.

Clara's sleeping. With her sunglasses on.

I place roses in a vase on the windowsill and sit in the armchair next to her bed.

There's no let-up in the heat. North Wales seems the same as South. No dramatic build-up and pour-down of rain to ease the tension. I've seen the long-range forecast: more heat.

I can't stand it.

But I know I have to.

I listen to Clara breathe.

The breaths in seem longer than the breaths out.

Ends.

National
Theatre
Wales

The nation of Wales is our stage. We collaborate with people and places to make extraordinary theatre that inspires change. From the intimate to the epic, our work is powerful, brave and unexpected. Created in Wales, with a global outlook, we are the English-language national theatre of Wales.

Our audiences have followed us and Michael Sheen around his hometown, Port Talbot, to watch *The Passion*, and returned to the town in 2017 for *We're Still Here*, a new production tackling the global steel crisis. Some partied with Neon Neon (Gruff Rhys & Boom Bip) in Cardiff, learning the extraordinary story of Italian publisher Giangiacomo Feltrinelli, in *Praxis Makes Perfect*. Hundreds climbed the foothills of Snowdon to hear poems by the National Poet of Wales, Gillian Clarke and witness first-hand the annual sheep-gathering, at *The Gathering/Yr Helfa*. Many watched a marathon, overnight performance of *Iliad* in Llanelli. People donned boots to experience *Mametz*, written by poet Owen Sheers and staged in farmland near Usk – the show offered a chilling glimpse of life and death in a WWI trench. More than 140,000 were in Cardiff to witness Roald Dahl's *City of the Unexpected*, Wales' biggest-ever arts event, staged to commemorate the writer's centenary on the streets of his hometown. And thousands joined us online for Tim Price's award-winning *The Radicalisation of Bradley Manning*, learning about a teenager in Pembrokeshire who grew to be one of the world's most influential and divisive political figures. Others watched across the world our live online broadcast of *Tide Whisperer* in Tenby, tackling the global phenomenon of displacement and mass movement.

These are just some of the sixty-plus productions we've staged on trains, military training grounds, beaches and mountains, in warehouses, nightclubs, cricket schools, tents, village halls, schools, aircraft hangars and libraries, all over towns like Barmouth, Laugharne, Rhyl and Aberystwyth, online and in apps, and in cities from Swansea to Tokyo.

www.nationaltheatrewales.org

Staff

TEAM Associate (Wrexham)	Iolanda Banu Viegas
Managing Director	Michelle Carwardine-Palmer
TEAM Coordinator	Naomi Chiffi
Head of Creative Development	Simon Coates
Head of Collaboration	Devinda De Silva
Head of Production	David Evans
Administrative Officer	Dom Farelli
Finance Coordinator (Maternity Cover)	Matthew Fisher
Head of Finance	Stephen Grant
Company Coordinator	Hannah John
Interim Press and PR Manager	Nia Jones
Campaigns Manager	Rhian Lewis
TEAM Assistant	Sophie Lewis
Executive Producer	Lisa Maguire
Finance Coordinator	Jenny McCarthy
Head of Development	Esther Morris
Live Events Apprentice	Kathryn Parker
Agency Coordinator	Gavin Porter
Interim Marketing Manager	Megan Price
Creative Associate	Marc Rees
TEAM Associate (Pembrokeshire)	Owain Roach
Development Coordinator	Alex Roberts
Casting Associate	Mawgaine Tarrant-Cornish
Production Assistant	Hadley Taylor
Artistic Director	Kully Thiarai
Associate Director	Julia Thomas
Producer	Martha Wilson

 Cymru Wales

 Cyngor Celfyddydau Cymru
Arts Council of Wales

 Noddir gan **Lywodraeth Cymru** Sponsored by **Welsh Government**

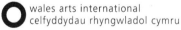 wales arts international
celfyddydau rhyngwladol cymru

ARIENNIR GAN Y LOTERI LOTTERY FUNDED

www.nickhernbooks.co.uk

 facebook.com/nickhernbooks

 twitter.com/nickhernbooks